A F·E·A·R ADVENTURE

THE SPACE PLAGUE

JAK SHADOW

Wizard Books

Published in the UK in 2005
by Wizard Books, an imprint of Icon Books Ltd.,
The Old Dairy, Brook Road, Thriplow,
Cambridge SG8 7RG
email: wizard@iconbooks.co.uk
www.iconbooks.co.uk/wizard

Sold in the UK, Europe, South Africa
and Asia by Faber and Faber Ltd.,
3 Queen Square, London WC1N 3AU
or their agents

Distributed in the UK, Europe, South Africa
and Asia by TBS Ltd., Frating Distribution Centre,
Colchester Road, Frating Green, Colchester CO7 7DW

Published in Australia in 2005
by Allen & Unwin Pty. Ltd.,
PO Box 8500, 83 Alexander Street,
Crows Nest, NSW 2065

Distributed in Canada by
Penguin Books Canada,
90 Eglinton Avenue East, Suite 700,
Toronto, Ontario M4P 2Y3

ISBN 1 84046 694 4

Contents

Introduction

Last summer you went to a holiday adventure camp. It was fantastic! Instead of teachers, real soldiers, explorers and athletes taught you how to do all kinds of things. You learned how to survive in dangerous lands, how to abseil down a mountain and how to crack secret codes. They even taught you how to track someone cross-country and how to avoid being followed.

On your last day at the adventure camp you were awarded five certificates and told that you were one of the best students they had ever had. You remember that final evening as if it were yesterday and now, with your dangerous mission about to begin, you replay every detail of the scene in your head.

★ ★ ★

After a last campfire and a meal in the open air, one of the sergeants whispers in your ear.

'Colonel Strong would like to see you in his

office. Please follow me. There is nothing to worry about; you haven't done anything wrong.'

You saw Colonel Strong on your first day. He is the officer in charge of the camp, a big man with a booming voice who is more than a little terrifying.

You cannot stop your knees from trembling, and your hands feel cold and clammy as you walk towards his office. You are wondering what on Earth he wants to talk about.

'My people have been watching you all week,' Colonel Strong begins. 'I know you have had a great time here and you've done extremely well. We are all very proud of what you have been able to achieve.'

'It seems that you are exactly what we are looking for. Sit yourself down and let me explain,' he says, pointing to the chair.

'The world is in great danger. More danger than you could possibly imagine,' the colonel continues.

Why is the colonel talking to you like this? He obviously has more to say so you wait for him to continue.

'My organisation is fighting a secret war against an evil alien genius.'

'But who is he and what does he want?' you ask.

'His name is Triton and he wants to rule the world,' the colonel tells you.

Colonel Strong passes you a photograph of Triton. He is like nothing you have ever seen before. He has green skin, piercing red eyes,  pointed ears, a large nose and has strange lumps on his face. You would have no trouble in picking him out in a crowd.

'I have checked out your history and I have watched you all week. I know that you are loyal, honest and brave, but even so I cannot tell you any more unless you swear a solemn oath to keep this secret.'

You are not too sure what the colonel means, but you know he is trustworthy and you long to hear more. You swear the solemn and binding oath that you will keep the secret.

'I work for an organisation called F.E.A.R.,' the colonel continues. 'It is an organisation so secret that only a handful of people in the whole world know about it.'

'But what is F.E.A.R.?' you ask.

'F.E.A.R. stands for Fighting Evil, Always Ready,' the colonel explains. 'I don't want you to feel you've been tricked but this activity camp was specially set up to recruit the ideal agent,' he continues. 'We selected only children who we knew would be brave, strong, honest and, above all, quick-witted. We have watched you this week, and out of all the children, you are the one we have picked. We want you to become a F.E.A.R. agent.'

'Agent! What sort of agent? A secret agent?' you shout.

'Yes, a very secret agent. But I can only tell you more if you agree to join us. Or would you prefer it if we just forgot this conversation?'

'Of course I want to help, but I'm only a child. What could I possibly do?' you ask.

'All of our agents are children now. Triton has captured all our best adult agents but he does not yet suspect our children.'

'Why can't we just hunt him down and kill him?' you reply.

'I wish it were that easy. The world Triton comes from is millions of miles from our planet, but somehow he has managed to get to Earth. He has a time machine and he is trying to change our time and our future. We have to stop him. We managed to capture one of his time machines and we've copied it so now we've got one of our own.'

'You can count on me,' you say, smiling at the colonel.

'If you agree to become a F.E.A.R. agent you will begin your training during the school holidays. You have been sworn to secrecy, and must not tell anyone about the work you are doing. We will tell your parents as much as they need to know, but no more.'

★ ★ ★

Over the holidays since, your training has been completed. You have worked hard and learned much. You know more about Triton now, especially the fact that he uses a time chip to take him back to a particular time and place. If you can take it from him, or destroy it, he will have to leave. F.E.A.R. have made a chip locator and on every mission you will take one with you. It will help you to find Triton.

Now you are ready to begin your mission, but Colonel Strong's words are ringing in your ears: 'Remember you are facing a most dangerous challenge and an evil enemy.'

You wait for your instructions.

How to Play

Before you start, the colonel will tell you as much as F.E.A.R. know about Triton's plans.

This is not like a normal book. Each section of the book is numbered. At the end of each section you will have a choice to make. Each of these choices will send you to a different section of the book. You make the choices and decide how you are going to deal with Triton.

If you fail, your mission will end and Triton will be able to continue his plan to take over the world. If you manage to combat all of the dangers Triton presents you will defeat him and the world will be safe – until he strikes in another time and another place! The world needs you.

Your Mission

Colonel Strong is waiting for you at the F.E.A.R. base camp gate when you pull up in the army jeep, driven by his sergeant, Harris. The colonel is arguing with someone on his mobile phone and you catch snatches of the conversation.

'Yes I understand that, but my agent must be 800 kilometres from Earth. He has to be there tomorrow. I'll wait to hear from you,' he shouts down the phone.

The colonel turns towards you and apologises. Your mind is racing. Eight hundred kilometres from Earth? A rocket? What is going on?

'Triton has struck,' announces the colonel. 'This could possibly be a dangerous mission. Not only have you got to travel 600 years into the future, but you've also got to be able to travel halfway across the galaxy.'

'What is Triton trying to do?' you ask.

'Well, it is a very long story, but in 400 years' time humans will start travelling to other planets and making contact with alien races. Triton comes from a distant planet, and in the future our spacecraft are getting closer and closer to his home. He wants to stop us. He has let loose a terrible plague on a tiny colony called Rosetta. It is far away from Earth, beyond the planet Jupiter.' The colonel hands you a photograph of Triton in a spacesuit as he explains.

'What is so special about Rosetta? Why has he let a plague loose there and what can we do about it?' you ask the colonel.

'In 600 years' time humans will start to settle on Rosetta,' explains Strong. 'It is the furthest planet away from Earth that a colony can settle on, but Triton is worried because it is the closest planet to his own. One of Triton's spacecraft has attacked Rosetta with rockets; inside them is a plague that can infect only humans. Triton hopes that the plague will spread and deal with the human race forever. He does not want humans settling close to his home. We can't let him get away with this.'

'Do we have anything that can stop the plague?' you ask.

'Yes, one of our agents managed to get to Rosetta and bring back a sample,' the colonel tells you. 'Our scientists have been working on it for several days and we think we have found a cure. We'd like you to deliver it to Rosetta.'

'So that's what you were talking about on the telephone,' you say.

'Yes. You'll be the youngest person ever to travel into space,' Strong explains. 'We've arranged for you to be on an emergency flight from the European Spaceport in South America. We need to get the time machine onto the rocket so that we can send you into the future. You'll appear in a space city that is orbiting the Earth in 600 years' time. There's an aircraft waiting to take us to the spaceport.

We've arranged for it to be refuelled over the Atlantic Ocean.'

Colonel Strong jumps into Harris's jeep with you and you roar off through the base, towards the waiting plane. It is huge and dozens of men are loading crates and boxes up the ramp at the back. Harris drives the jeep straight into the cargo hold of the aircraft. The flight is nearly ready to leave. Colonel Strong is barking orders at his men and at the last minute a truck arrives, full of scientists and technicians who will need to set up the time machine on the rocket.

Colonel Strong finally finishes briefing his men when you are over the Atlantic Ocean and heading for South America. This sounds like a very complicated mission and you wonder why the humans in the future have not been able to make their own cure for the plague. You ask the colonel.

'It's a very old disease and we think Triton found it in Egypt,' he replies. 'The humans in the future have no idea what it is, but we've managed to work it out and make a cure.'

'Won't I catch the plague straight away?' you ask.

'No', replies the colonel. 'We're going to have to inject you with the cure. That should protect you from it. It worked on Agent 214 who collected the sample, although he was quite ill until we managed to make the cure.'

The thought of an injection doesn't exactly thrill you, and you look away as one of the scientists injects the cure into your arm. It makes you feel a little bit dizzy, but at least you are now protected against the plague and you are ready for your mission.

Now read paragraph **1** to begin your adventure.

The Space Plague

1

The aircraft flies straight into the European Spaceport on the coast overlooking the Atlantic Ocean. Hundreds of people are waiting to help unload the aircraft and get the rocket ready for lift-off. Harris drives you and Colonel Strong straight to Mission Control. You are taken into a room to make your last preparations before the flight.

'I've got to give you three things,' says the colonel.

He passes you a small test tube that has a yellowy-green, oily liquid in it. This must be the cure to the plague. You place it on the table.

'I know it doesn't look like there is much, but you don't have to inject it into someone who has the plague. You just need to be able to get it into the air that people are breathing. If, for example, you pour it into the air conditioning that would work. It is very fast acting,' the colonel explains.

While the colonel is explaining the cure he hands you a piece of plastic that looks a bit like a credit card. It has your photograph on it.

'This is your passport and payment card,' he says. 'We've put 50,000 galactic credits on it, which is more than enough to cover anything you might have to pay for.'

'Thanks, I bet they've got some really great computer games in the future,' you joke with the colonel. But he just ignores you and continues talking.

'Here's the chip locator. You just flick it on and it should tell you where Triton is. When you find him you must place the chip in the locator to banish Triton from that time.' He hands  you a device that looks a bit like a mobile phone. 'We've got three other things, but you only have room to take one of them. Firstly, there's a universal translator. If you have one of these then you'll be able to understand any language and any

alien will be able to understand you.'

You look at the other two objects.

One of them is an oxygen mask, which could be useful for breathing in space. The last object is a pair of boots that seem to be very heavy when you pick them up.

'They are magnetic boots. There may be times when you are so light that you won't be able to stay on the ground.

These boots will allow you to walk,' Colonel Strong tells you.

If you wish to choose the universal translator, go to **58**. If you prefer the oxygen mask, go to **66**. If you think the magnetic boots would be the most useful, go to **12**.

2

The alien with the crab claws grabs your arm with one of his pincers. His other claw cuts through your pocket and picks out the test tube. A terrible smile spreads across his face. 'You must be a F.E.A.R. agent,' he says. He lets you go, steps back and drops the test tube on the floor, grinding it under his foot.

'So much for F.E.A.R.,' he says, and the other two aliens laugh.

Strange shapes pass before your eyes and you feel yourself falling, falling, falling.

You find yourself on the floor of the time chamber and see Colonel Strong's face peering through the glass. Your mission is over. Strong promised that you would not come to any harm and he has kept his promise. The colonel opens the door and helps you to your feet.

'It seems I've failed. I should have tried to get away. But we could try it all again, couldn't we?' you say.

If you would like to try the mission once again, go back to **1**.

3

It is unlucky that you didn't choose to bring your magnetic boots. Now there is no easy way of getting to the mini-ship.

'The captain will turn off the oxygen and power up the gravity,' Simon tells you.

This will work if you have your oxygen mask. If you have an oxygen mask then go to **91**. If you don't have your oxygen mask you should go to **24**.

4

You continue to pull yourself along the corridor, but it is getting more difficult to breathe. Now that the fans have been turned off there is very little oxygen. You can hear a clunking sound and you look out of the window to see another ship parked alongside Captain Harry's starship. You begin to feel very dizzy and tired. The last thing you see is Triton's face at one of the windows of the other starship. Triton has beaten you this time. Perhaps next time you'll be able to get to Rosetta and save the settlers. Suddenly strange shapes pass before your eyes and you feel yourself falling, falling, falling.

You find yourself on the floor of the time chamber and see Colonel Strong's face peering through the glass. Your mission is over. Strong promised that you would not come to any harm and he has kept his promise. The colonel opens the door and helps you to your feet.

'It seems we've failed. I shouldn't have fallen for that. I should have realised it was a trap. We could try it all again, couldn't we?' you say.

If you would like to try the mission once again, go back to **1**.

5

You decide to make a break for it, but it is a pretty uneven match as he is in a truck and you're on foot. In a minute or two he will have caught up with you. You can hear his booming voice telling the driver to go faster and run you over. Just ahead you can see a cave in the rocks. Do you want to head for it? If so, go to **82**. Or do you think that you would be better off continuing to run and hope that you can outpace him? If so, go to **52**.

6

You head towards the observation deck, which has a huge sweep of windows, giving you a wonderful view of the space station. The starship's journey is already underway, and in just a few minutes the space station is a tiny speck in the distance and you can see Earth thousands of miles below you.

You decide to keep walking, dodging between groups of aliens and humans. They are all gazing out at the stars. You lose sight of the three alien agents and double back to head for your room. You press your key and it gives you instructions all the way there. When you get to the door it opens automatically. Now you can settle down and order some food and drink from the electronic food bar. Turn to **56**.

7

The space map is vast and covers nearly a whole wall, but it is clear enough to understand. You can see Earth and there is a line stretching out to all of the planets, including Jupiter. You look at the area around Jupiter more closely and see that there is a pink line that runs between Jupiter and Rosetta. But what does the pink line mean? You look down at the key and it says 'monthly service only'. You hope that you might be able to catch a connecting flight soon.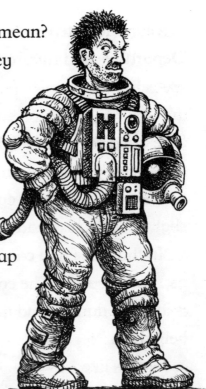

While you are concentrating on the map a rather scruffy looking man has come over to stand next to you. He does not seem particularly interested in the map but is more interested in what you are looking at.

'Thinking of going to Rosetta? I wouldn't if I were you. There's a plague on the planet and it is out of bounds.'

If you want to talk to the man then turn to **45**. If you think he is being a little too nosey for his own good, or your own, then you should leave immediately to head for the Galactic Departures and turn to **37**.

8

'I've got a cure for the plague and I must get it to Rosetta', you explain.

The captain's fishy eyes narrow and he slightly turns his head as if he is thinking.

'In that case you can definitely come with us,' he whispers. 'The colony on the planet is in great danger and you can obviously help them.'

It looks like you will be joining them on the trip to Rosetta. Go to **81**.

9

Just ahead of you is a shop and you slip inside to hide behind one of the displays. The display is a large model of a green alien with yellow eyes and warts all over its face. Beside it is a box full of little, round disks. On each disk 'Jak

Shadow III's Space Plague 8' is written. This must be what people in this time have instead of books.

While you are looking at the display, three odd-looking aliens enter the shop. One is a tall creature who is grey and like a beanpole. He has two enormous eyes on the end of stalks, which are swivelling around and around looking for you. The second alien is barely a metre tall, with a huge, orange nose poking out of his blue fur. The third alien looks the most dangerous: instead of hands, he has claws like a crab and at least five pairs of eyes, all bright red.

All three of them are looking around the shop to try and find you.

'Jupiter flight leaves in ten minutes. All remaining passengers report to Gate 562,' announces the tannoy system.

Will you risk leaving the shop to head for Gate 562 to catch a flight to Jupiter? If so, go to **47**. If you think it is too risky and you should remain in the shop, go to **63**.

10

You pass the group of humans and no sooner have you done so than the key speaks again and says, 'The second door on your left is room 1071. Thank you for choosing our Intergalactic Service.'

The door opens automatically when you reach it and as you walk in you feel something grab your shoulder. You spin around and see one of the aliens that has been following you. A smile spreads across his face and he pushes you into the room.

'Seems to me you've found a cure. I'll take your test tube,' he snarls at you. You do not have a choice, so you hand it over to him. By now the other two agents have joined him.

'Let's finish him here,' says one of them.

Suddenly strange shapes pass before your eyes and you feel yourself falling, falling, falling. You find yourself on the floor of the time chamber and see Colonel Strong's face peering through the glass. Your mission is over.

Strong promised that you would not come to any harm and he has kept his promise. The colonel opens the door and helps you to your feet.

'It seems we've failed. Perhaps I shouldn't have let them know where my room was. But we could try it all again, couldn't we?' you suggest.

If you would like to try the mission once again, go back to **1**.

11

While Triton's agents are buying their tickets and asking the pink and green alien about you, you take the chance to head for the boarding gate. The flashing board over your head tells you that you have just five minutes to get onboard before the starship leaves. You manage to get to the boarding gate and are whisked down a tube towards the starship, where a tall, yellow and blue striped alien with eight arms meets you.

'Please report to the passenger desk and you will be given a room,' the alien smiles.

With one last look behind, you see the three agents coming down the tube towards you. Now turn to **13**.

12

You will be helpless if there is no gravity. You will just be floating around, so the magnetic boots could be very useful.

'I think I'll take the magnetic boots, even though they are heavy,' you say.

'You'll need to know that the magnet will only work on metal, so they can be used in a spaceship or a space station but not in space. You just need to press the button on the left boot to turn them on,' Colonel Strong explains.

You pull on a jumpsuit and zip it up. Carefully you put the plague cure in one of the top pockets and zip that up. You then put on the magnetic boots, which are surprisingly light now that you have them on your feet. Colonel

Strong passes you the chip locator, which you put into another pocket.

You are now ready to go and it will soon be time for the rocket to blast off and take you into outer space. Now go to **79**.

13

Just ahead is a reception desk. Behind the desk is a human. He is wearing a tie but he doesn't have a shirt and he is moving in the weirdest way. As you get closer you can see he is a very strange creature. The top of his body looks human, but the rest of him is a horse. 'Welcome aboard the Star Cruise Ship. How can I help you?' he asks.

'I'd like a room,' you reply.

'Certainly. Economy or First Class?'

'I think I'll go for First Class,' you say, thinking about the payment card Colonel Strong gave you.

'Of course,' he says, with his hand reaching out for your card.

He slips it into a slot in the desk, and a bright yellow key comes out of a hole in front of you. The creature hands you back your card and tells you that your room number is 1071.

The spaceship is incredible. It is like a vast hotel. There are at least three swimming pools, one full of water for humans and the other two filled with liquid so poisonous to humans that they can only be used by the aliens.

All the time Triton's three agents are watching you. If you want to head straight for your room then go to **80**. If you think you should try to lose them and then double back to your room go to **6**.

14

You manage to get the oxygen mask out of your pocket and fix the straps around your head. At least you will be able to breathe even if you can't walk! You continue to drag yourself along the corridor then you hear a clunking sound. You look out of a window to see that another ship has stopped alongside Captain Harry's spaceship. A tube is joining the two ships together.

Perhaps Triton or his agents are following you? If you want to head for the door where the tube is connected to investigate, turn to **15**. If you think you would be safer hiding until you know who has entered the ship, turn to **67**.

15

You head off towards the tube as quickly as possible. As you turn the last corner of the corridor you bump into a large, green shape. It nearly knocks you over and as you look up you see the smiling face of Triton who you recognise from the photo that Strong showed you.

'A F.E.A.R. agent if I'm not mistaken! So the humans are using children now, are they? Well, you fell into my trap very easily, didn't you?' he sneers.

'Triton, you'll never get away with this,' you shout.

'Oh but I will. You see, Captain Harry isn't really a human. He is from a completely different planet and has two hearts, three lungs and a brain twice the size of any human being. I am just delivering the latest batch of plague for him. He is going to take these to all of the planets where you humans have settled. In just a few weeks there will be no more humans and then the galaxy will be mine!'

Triton levels a gun at you, but before he can fire you see strange shapes pass before your eyes and you feel yourself falling, falling, falling.

You find yourself on the floor of the time chamber and see Colonel Strong's face peering through the glass. Your mission is over. Strong promised that you would not come to any harm and he has kept his promise. The colonel opens the door and helps you to your feet.

'It seems we've failed. We could try it all again, couldn't we? I can't believe I fell into that trap so easily,' you say.

If you would like to try the mission once again, go back to **1**.

16

'We're not going to outrun them! Where can we hide?' you shout to Simon.

'There's an asteroid belt about two minutes ahead. We'll head there and see if we can lose them,' he shouts back.

The asteroid belt is full of huge tumbling and spinning rocks. Most of them are bigger than the starship. While you are looking out of the window at all of the asteroids you realise one is heading straight for the ship.

'Quick, get into the gun turret and fire,' screams Simon.

Now turn to **90**.

17

You grab the controls and steer the mini-ship down through the last few hundred metres, heading for the closest place to the colony to land. The planet's surface is extremely rocky and it is now too late to change your mind and land somewhere flatter. The underneath of the mini-ship hits a jagged rock and it flips over, landing upside down.

Luckily, you manage to scramble out unhurt, but the mini-ship is wrecked. Hopefully if you complete your mission you won't need to leave the planet that way. Turn to **65**.

18

You stand still, arms folded, and wait for the truck to pull up. Triton steps out with two huge aliens.

'You're not going to get away with this,' you say to Triton. 'I'm going to stop you.'

'I don't think so,' he replies.

The two henchmen raise their guns and as

they squeeze the triggers you suddenly see strange shapes pass before your eyes and you feel yourself falling, falling, falling.

You find yourself on the floor of the time chamber and see Colonel Strong's face peering through the glass. Your mission is over. Strong promised that you would not come to any harm and he has kept his promise. The colonel opens the door and helps you to your feet.

'It seems we've failed. I shouldn't have tried to face Triton like that, I could never have beaten him. But we could try it all again, couldn't we?'

If you would like to try the mission once again, go back to **1**.

19

You search the ship until you find a sign that says 'emergency escape pods'. Perhaps this is where you will find a mini-ship?

You turn down a corridor and suddenly you can hear footsteps. You hide inside a room that

has a circular window in the door. You see
two alien creatures that look like giant, red rats
walk past. They have sharp teeth and beady
eyes and are heavily armed with guns and
other weapons. One of them stops and sniffs the
air. 'Human? Yummy!' he says, amazing you
that he can speak English.

'I'm hungry too, Snarl, but I don't want to
think about food. Come on, we've got work to
do!' the other creature replies.

The two rat men disappear up the corridor and you carefully open the door and head towards the emergency pods. One of them is ready, so you jump inside and press the power button to charge up the engines. You look at the controls and see that the computer speaks thousands of different languages. You check along the panel and see a button with 'Planet Earth' written on it. A computer screen flickers into action and a voice asks you where you want to go.

'Jupiter,' you reply.

'Destination Jupiter. Confirmed,' it replies.

With that, a door of the spaceship opens and the mini-ship blasts off into space towards Jupiter. Go to **88**.

20

You continue walking past many sickly colonists, but there is no sign of a doctor or a nurse. You reach the end of the passageway and it branches to the left and to the right. Which way will you go? If you want to turn left, go to **31**. If you want to turn right, go to **75**.

21

You decide to run and you scramble through the rocks, hoping to get away from Triton and his henchmen. About 20 metres ahead is a cave entrance. Do you want to run towards it? If so, go to **82**. If you think it would be better to continue running, go to **33**.

22

You decide that you need to stop the rest of these missiles from being taken onto Captain Harry's ship. Heaven knows what Triton has got in mind. Perhaps he intends to destroy every human? If you can somehow stop these missiles from getting onto Captain Harry's ship then you can save millions of humans.

You run back towards the tube and as you reach it you hear voices and see Triton and his men returning to his starship to collect another batch of missiles.

Do you want to continue to try and stop the missiles from entering Captain Harry's ship? If so, go to **61**. If you think that Triton and his men are too strong for you and want to try to get to Rosetta then you need to escape from Triton's starship in a mini-ship. Go to **19**.

23

You manage to find a huge metal bar, which you can barely carry. This should do the trick. With difficulty, you stagger towards the water tank and smash the side with the metal bar. You hit it three times before it cracks and you quickly jump out of the way as water gushes through the hole.

The water pours through the streets and smashes against Triton's tanks. Some of them burst into flames and others flip over. You have managed to stop him and the people will be safe for the time being. But now you need to find a doctor, so you head back towards the corridor. Go to 75.

24

'No magnetic boots and no oxygen mask,' says Simon. 'Here, take my mask. I'm sure I can hold my breath for two minutes. You'll have to be quick though. As soon as I open that door – run!'

You take Simon's oxygen mask, thank him and the starfish and run towards the mini-ship as soon as the door opens. Once onboard the mini-ship you press the starter button and a computer screen flickers into action.

'Destination?' it asks.

'Take me down to the surface of the planet Rosetta,' you order.

'Confirmed,' the computer replies.

With that the mini-ship's engines blast off and you whizz into space then turn towards the planet. You are moving at a terrific speed and in seconds you can see Rosetta in front of you.

'Exact destination?' asks the computer.

'Near the colony,' you reply.

The mini-ship speeds through the atmosphere, through the clouds and then you can see the rocky surface of the planet beneath you. Will you try to land close to the colony, even though this means that you will land on very rocky ground? If so, go to **17**. Or will you try to land further away on flatter ground? If so, go to **46**.

25

'Excuse me,' you begin, 'I couldn't help overhearing that you're going to Rosetta.'

There's a short pause as the translator speaks to the starfish in his own language. He turns around to face you and has cold, fishy eyes. 'Yes I am,' you hear through your translator.

'I wondered if you had room for me. I've, erm, got family on the planet. Erm, my uncle, he's there,' you lie.

'I don't believe that for one minute. Why do you really want to go to Rosetta? It is not exactly the best place for a holiday.'

Will you tell him why you really want to go to the planet? If so, go to **8**. If you decide not to tell him, go to **71**.

26

As Triton's communicator reaches his lips you use one of your special F.E.A.R. kicks to knock it out of his hand. It smashes against the wall. Triton growls and fires his gun at you, but it misses and hits one of his own men.

Even now Triton could still stop you. Will you try to grab his gun? If so, go to **28**. Or will you try and hide away from him? If so, go to **69**.

27

You slip your hand into your pocket and with one of your fingers you push the test tube into the sleeve of your jumpsuit. Then you put your hands behind your back and hold the test tube tightly. Luckily the guard only scans the front of you and his wand doesn't go off.

'On you go,' he says.

'That was close,' you think, and smile at the two-headed man as you walk through the barrier. As you continue you are aware that the

three aliens you spotted earlier are following
you. One is a tall creature, who is grey and like
a beanpole. He has two enormous eyes on the
end of stalks, which are swivelling around and
around looking for you. The second alien is
barely a metre tall and has an orange nose
poking out of his blue fur. The third alien looks
the most dangerous. Instead of hands he has
claws like a crab and at least five pairs of bright
red eyes. Now turn to **97**.

28

You grab the gun and try to fire at Triton. The gun is broken and will not work, so you throw it at him. It hits him on the arm and rips his spacesuit. He spins around, groaning, moaning and spluttering. You stand over him.

'Give me the time chip,' you shout at him. He has no choice but to hand it over. You drop it to the floor and grind it into the ground under your boot. You have beaten him! Turn to **100**.

29

You are not sure whether or not the starfish can understand English. Do you have your universal translator? If you do, turn to **25**. If you do not have the translator then turn to **62**.

30

'Can you make this thing fly any faster?' you shout.

Simon smiles and translates what you have said to the captain, then tells you the reply: 'We're already pulling away from them. They'll never keep up with us – this is an incredibly powerful ship.'

Simon and the starfish are true to their word and gradually Triton's starship slips further behind until it is a speck in the distance. In a few short hours you are within sight of Rosetta.

Suddenly, out of nowhere, an alien ship swings into view, firing as it turns to attack you.

'Triton!' you and Simon shout, both at the same time.

'Quickly, get in the gun turret,' shouts Simon. 'Fire at him as he comes around.'

You climb up a ladder into a small dome and sit behind a huge blaster. You press a green button and the gun powers up, ready to fire. The alien ship is almost on top of you. Will you shoot straight at it? If so, go to **74**. Or will you fire just ahead of the ship? If so, go to **50**.

31

You decide to turn left and walk for a few more minutes. You see hundreds of colonists lying on the ground. You feel awful because there is nothing you can do for them at the moment. The corridor ends and opens out into a huge underground space, full of buildings. It is like a city centre, and there are sick people everywhere.

As you are walking towards the main street you can hear engines in the distance. Perhaps someone else has come to help the colonists? But then you hear explosions and screams. You run into a building, climb to the top floor and look out of the window. You see that Triton is leading an army of tanks through the city,

firing at everything. The people must be saved! Triton's tanks have already reached the central square of the city.

Will you run back through the corridors to try and find a doctor? If so, go to **75**. Or will you try to stop Triton now? If so, go to **84**.

32

You decide to follow the starfish and after a few minutes he stands up and walks out of the Captain's Bar followed by the human. You get the feeling that they are shipmates and that the man works for the starfish. They don't seem to be in any particular hurry, but they walk for a long time, past several docks full of starships of various shapes and sizes. Eventually they stop outside a bank.

The starfish slips inside the bank and his crewman waits outside. You decide to walk up to him and ask for a lift to Rosetta.

'I need to go to Rosetta to see my uncle,' you tell him.

'A likely story,' he replies. 'No one wants to go to Rosetta. It is a miserable place and there is plague there.'

'I know that,' you say, 'but I have to get to the planet.'

'Well, I suppose you'd better follow us as soon as the captain has finished his business,' he tells you.

Turn to **81**.

33

Ignoring the cave, you continue to run. Triton and his men are gaining on you. You hear Triton scream 'Fire!' and suddenly strange shapes pass before your eyes. You feel yourself falling, falling, falling.

You find yourself on the floor of the time chamber and see Colonel Strong's face peering through the glass. Your mission is over. Strong promised that you would not come to any harm and he has kept his promise. The colonel opens the door and helps you to your feet.

'It seems I've failed. I had no chance of outrunning them. But we could try it all again, couldn't we?' you suggest to the colonel.

If you would like to try the mission once again, go back to **1**.

34

You land with a bit of a thump on the floor of the orbiting space station. Luckily, this part of the space station is not very busy and nobody seems to have noticed you as everyone is walking in the direction signposted 'Galactic Departures'. You think 'walk' and then you realise that some of them are not walking at all. Just a few feet away there is a very strange looking creature. It is about the size of a car and has at least eight eyes and a trunk, rather like an elephant. It is floating along. Beyond this alien is a family from another far-off planet. They look like giant slugs and are leaving a slimy trail behind them.

You walk over towards one of the many windows and look out. Almost as far as the eye can see there are tubes and globes, all joined to one another. Around each of the globes are starships. This is not so much a space station as an orbiting city, and it is huge.

You really need to know where Rosetta is and how you might be able to get there. A few metres away from you is a space map, which looks rather like a bus or train map. It connects planets and space stations around the galaxy. If you would like to have a look at this then turn to 7. Or you could go to the Galactic Departures area. If so, turn to **37**.

35

You slip in amongst the crowd of humans and although your key is telling you that you are walking in the wrong direction, Triton's three alien agents pass you by without even looking at you. You leave the humans to head off to the restaurant and double back. This time you manage to get to your room without being spotted.

The door opens automatically in front of you and you walk into room 1071. The first thing you do is double lock the door then settle down for a well-earned rest and some food and drink from the electronic food bar. Now turn to **56**.

36

'I'm not sure I should go with you, I don't know you,' you tell the stranger.

'You've nothing to fear from me. I've been flying between planets for the past 40 years. Everyone knows me. But if you don't trust me I'll understand. You won't get to Rosetta any other way though, not from here,' he tells you.

You wonder whether he is right. If you want to change your mind and go with the stranger, turn to **64**. If you think you are better off without him, turn to **95**.

37

You walk towards the sign marked 'Galactic Departures' and pass through a security station. A bright yellow alien, with bony spikes instead of hair sticking out of his head, is staring at a computer screen. As you pass by you can see your skeleton on the screen in front of him. You walk a few more steps and a voice asks: 'Destination?'

'Galactic Departures,' you reply.

A part of the floor underneath your feet lifts up and you are whisked along the corridor into a huge dome. It is full of humans and aliens, and all of them are on strange floating platforms like you. Your platform stops and disappears into the ground just beside the departures board. You look around and see what must be 50 or 60 different aliens and then you see something that makes your heart sink.

A green creature, with warts all over its face, is standing no more than ten metres from you. It must be Triton! You slip your hand into your pocket, turn on your chip locator and walk slowly towards him. It doesn't buzz. So perhaps it isn't Triton. You remember you are close to his planet so it may just be another alien from his home. The creature turns around and spots you and shuffles off. As you follow him you feel the hairs on the back of your neck begin to stand on end and you can see several different alien creatures moving towards you. Perhaps they have nothing to do with Triton and they are just galactic tourists on holiday, but maybe they are Triton's agents?

Will you try to find somewhere to hide? If so, go to **9**. Or will you go to the ticket desk and book yourself on a flight to Rosetta? If so, go to **85**.

38

You've still got a couple of hundred metres between you and the truck and you manage to cover quite a distance before they spot you. Just ahead is a rocky hill, which looks like it is the start of a mountain range. You clamber through the rocks, knowing that the truck cannot follow you there.

Off to your left you see a shining, steel door. This must be a way to get to the colony, so you run towards it. The door has a button and beside that a keypad. You press the button, hoping that someone will answer.

'Nai? Auriste?' you hear. 'Dessera, Efta, Dessera, Efta.'

What on Earth can this mean? Have you got a universal translator with you? If so, turn to **48**. If you do not have a universal translator then turn to **92**.

39

The security guard's wand sweeps over the pocket in which you are hiding the test tube. It starts to buzz!

'Alert! Alert!' shouts the guard.

His other hand reaches out and grabs you by the shoulder. In seconds three other guards are beside you.

'You're under arrest,' one of them tells you.

They take you to the cells and no sooner have they locked the door than you suddenly see strange shapes pass before your eyes and you feel yourself falling, falling, falling.

You find yourself on the floor of the time chamber and see Colonel Strong's face peering through the glass. Your mission is over. Strong promised that you would not come to any harm and he has kept his promise. The colonel opens the door and helps you to your feet.

'It seems we've failed. I should have hidden the test tube. But we could try it all again, couldn't we?' you say.

If you would like to try the mission once again, go back to **1**.

40

You manage to reach down and turn on your magnetic boots, and in a second or two they drag you down towards the floor. You land with a clunk. It is really quite easy to walk in the boots so you head off down the corridor, hoping that you can find the flight control room.

As the ship is not very big, you find the flight control room quite easily. There's no sound and no one around. The room is empty. There is no sign of Captain Harry or any of the crew. Turn to **53**.

41

Without any warning you leap on Triton. You manage to get him onto the floor and he is trying to reach for his gun, which has fallen out of his hand.

If you think you can handle Triton alone then go to **72**. If you think you need help then you should shout for it now. Go to **89**.

42

You walk straight up to the purple alien and try to pass him. He blocks your way with three of his tentacles and points three guns at you.

'Blaag, stog appoloy,' seems to be what he says.

'Pardon?' you ask.

'Blaag, stog appoloy,' he shouts, more loudly.

'OK then,' you say, and walk past him.

You make your way down the tube and into Triton's ship. There are stacks of boxes marked 'poison' but no sign of any of his men. Perhaps you can find a mini-ship and escape from Triton's starship? If you want to do this, turn to **19**. Or you could hide for the time being and hope that you are not captured. Turn to **98**.

43

'Help, help! He's not a real doctor. Somebody help me!' you scream.

'No one is strong enough to help you,' laughs the doctor. But he is wrong. A man lying on the floor grabs the fake doctor's legs. As the doctor is struggling, you wind an enormous bandage around and around him until he looks like a mummy. He can't move and he just falls to the ground, groaning.

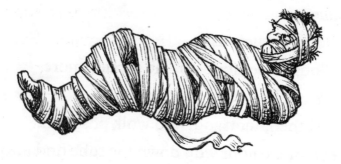

'If you've really got the cure, open up the air conditioning and pour it inside,' says the man who grabbed the fake doctor's legs.

You do this immediately and then step back. In just a few minutes the people start to sit up. It seems that the cure must have worked.

'My name is John Chard and I'm the leader of the colonists,' says the man who helped you. 'I don't know how to thank you.'

Suddenly you hear a crashing sound and Triton appears at the doorway.

'You might have cured them,' he yells, 'but I'll finish you!' With that, Triton grabs his gun and aims it at you. Turn to 77.

44

You flatten yourself against the door and hope that Triton and his men will not spot you. But they begin firing wildly in your direction and you hear one of the blasters hit the rocks above your head. There is a groaning noise and a huge lump of stone falls towards you. Suddenly strange shapes pass before your eyes and you feel yourself falling, falling, falling.

You find yourself on the floor of the time chamber and see Colonel Strong's face peering through the glass. Your mission is over. Strong promised that you would not come to any harm and he has kept his promise. The colonel opens the door and helps you to your feet.

'It seems I've failed. If only I had a universal translator I would have understood that the door's computer was telling me the code. We could try it all again, couldn't we?' you ask the colonel.

If you would like to try the mission once again, go back to **1**.

45

'Yes I do want to go to Rosetta – my family is there,' you lie to the strange-looking man.

'Really?' he replies. 'You are in luck. I happen to be passing by Rosetta. I'm heading for some of the outer planets. Do you want a lift?'

The man seems a little too willing to help you and he hasn't even asked you to pay for the trip. If you wish to go with him, turn to **64**. If you think you would be safer travelling with a lot more people, turn to **36**.

46

You grab the controls of the mini-ship and steer it through the last few hundred metres to the surface. You sweep over a rocky area and then

see some flat sand up ahead. You manage to land perfectly and climb out of the mini-ship to look around. The colony is some way off and you need to get there as soon as possible. Go to **65**.

47

You sprint forward, catching the three aliens that have been following you by surprise. The alien with the crab claws snaps at your arm but you are too quick for it. In a second you are outside the shop and heading towards the departure gate. You then see a long line of alien schoolchildren. They are from lots of different alien races, and are being led towards the gate by two creatures that look like giant Easter eggs, with tiny legs and long, thin arms.

You slip in among the schoolchildren, hoping that Triton's agents will not spot you.

You are now walking alongside a short, grey creature that looks a bit like a frog, but has hooves like a horse and long, wavy fingers that must be nearly half a metre long. The creature is trying to talk to you but you don't understand what it is saying. Do you have your universal translator? If you have the translator, go to **86**. If you do not have the translator, go to **73**.

48

You flick on the universal translator. Immediately it tells you that the door's computer is speaking in Greek. It is asking you to press in the entry code, which is 4747. You do this and the door slides open.

Inside is a terrible sight. There are people lying all over the floor, moaning and groaning. These must be the colonists that are suffering from the plague. There is nothing you can do

for any of them until you can find a doctor, so
this must be your next mission. Now go to **20**.

49

The three aliens lose sight of you as you dodge
behind a pillar and crouch down behind a
group of large aliens. You watch the agent with
the crab claws run straight past you and you
remain hidden for a while. When you get up
you cannot see any of the aliens. You notice a
flashing sign that says 'Captain's Bar' and
think this could be a great place to find a lift to
Rosetta. Turn to **83**.

50

Firing ahead of the alien ship was a good choice. By the time the rays of your blaster reach the ship it has moved position. It spins out of control and disappears into space.

'Great shot!' shouts Simon. 'Now let's get you down to Rosetta.'

You will have to use a mini-ship to land on Rosetta, but it is located in a part of the ship that doesn't have any gravity. Do you have magnetic boots? If you do have magnetic boots, go to **78**. If you do not have magnetic boots, go to **3**.

51

Gerda waves its wispy hands at you to say goodbye as the teachers lead the children down one of the corridors. You wave back and wonder what to do next.

You look behind to see if you are still being followed and sure enough Triton's three alien agents are slowly walking towards you. Now turn to **13**.

52

You decide to continue running, but the truck is gaining on you. You hide behind a rock to catch your breath and then carry on towards the colony. Go to **38**.

53

As you look around the control room you realise that none of the control panels are working. It seems as if the power to the ship has been turned off. You cannot even hear the low humming of the engines.

You are thinking about what to do next when suddenly you hear a loud clunking noise. You look out of the main window of the control room and see that another starship has stopped alongside Captain Harry's ship. A tube joins the two ships together. Perhaps someone has come to save you? Or perhaps this has been a trap all along?

If you want to head for the tube and see who it is on the other starship, go to **15**. If you think it would be better to hide for the time being and see what happens, go to **67**.

54

You turn to run, but trip over a sick woman who is lying on the floor. The fake doctor looms over you and stamps his foot down on your arm so you cannot get away.

He stands over you with a tiny bottle in his hand. 'I'll just drop a little of this liquid into your mouth,' he says. 'Even your cure won't save you now.' This must have an even worse plague in it! He unscrews the bottle and begins to tip it towards your mouth. Suddenly strange shapes pass before your eyes and you feel yourself falling, falling, falling.

You find yourself on the floor of the time chamber and see Colonel Strong's face peering through the glass. Your mission is over. Strong promised that you would not come to any harm and he has kept his promise. The colonel opens the door and helps you to your feet.

'It seems I've failed. But I was so close to completing the mission,' you say.

If you would like to try the mission once again, go back to **1**.

55

'Make sure no one else comes through this door after me. There's a dangerous alien loose on the ship,' you say to the purple creature, hoping that it speaks English.

'OK, then,' it replies.

You walk past the alien, unable to stop yourself from smiling. You walk along the tube and into Triton's ship. There are stacks of boxes marked 'poison' but no sign of any of his men. Perhaps you can find a mini-ship and escape from Triton's starship? You have no idea how many of Triton's men are onboard

the starship. You could search for a mini-ship; if so go to **19**. Or you could hide for the time being and hope that you are not captured. If so, go to **98**.

56

It takes just over two days to get to Jupiter. You can't help but think that the three alien agents are still hunting around the ship for you.

You enjoy your last breakfast from the electronic food bar and as you leave your room you find a package on the floor outside your door. You pick it up and tear it open. Inside is a Jupiter guidebook and a universal translator!

You enter the main deck of the starship and there are thousands of creatures hanging around, waiting to get off the ship. You spot Triton's three agents before they see you.

Do you want to risk leaving the starship with the rest of the passengers? If so, go to **76**. If you think it would be safer to try and find a way to slip out of the ship with the luggage, turn to **68**.

57

You fire for a second time and miss the alien ship again. This time it fires several rockets at your ship and you hear huge explosions as they strike you. Your ship begins to spin out of control and below you there is fire. Suddenly strange shapes pass before your eyes and you feel yourself falling, falling, falling.

You find yourself on the floor of the time chamber and see Colonel Strong's face peering through the glass. Your mission is over. Strong promised that you would not come to any harm and he has kept his promise. The colonel opens the door and helps you to your feet.

'It seems I've failed. Perhaps I should have fired ahead of the alien ship. But we could try it all again, couldn't we?' you ask the colonel.

If you would like to try the mission once again, go back to **1**.

58

The universal translator could
be very useful. At least you
will be able to understand
what people are saying
and be able to talk to them.
It is a good choice because

you have no idea who you might need to have a
conversation with.

'I think I'll take the universal translator,' you
say.

'That's a good choice. Although many aliens
speak English, a lot of them do not and there is
no way of knowing whether you might need to
talk to an alien pilot during your mission,'
replies the colonel.

You pull on a jumpsuit and zip it up. It has
many pockets, which you fill with the items you
need to take. Carefully, you put the plague
cure in one of the top pockets and zip that up.
You then safely place the universal translator
into another pocket. Colonel Strong passes you

the chip locator, which you put into another pocket.

You are now ready to go and it will soon be time for the rocket to blast off and take you into outer space. Go to **79**.

59

You manage to make it to the mini-ship and climb onboard. You press the starter button and a computer screen flickers into action.

'Destination?' it asks.

'Take me down to the surface of the planet Rosetta,' you order.

With that the mini-ship's engines blast off and you whizz into space. You are moving at a terrific speed and in seconds you can see Rosetta in front of you.

'Exact destination?'

'Get me near the colony,' you say.

'Confirmed.'

The mini-ship speeds through the atmosphere, through the clouds and then you can see the rocky surface of the planet beneath you. Will you try to land close to the colony, even though this means that you will land on very rocky ground? If so, go to **17**. Or will you land further away on flatter ground? If so, go to **46**.

60

If anything, the Jupiter space station is even bigger than the one orbiting Earth. You spot hundreds of different aliens who must come from all over the universe. Your first goal must be to find some way of getting to Rosetta. You head for the main departure point, which is full of humans and aliens.

There is a security guard up ahead. You could ask him where you need to go to catch a ship to Rosetta. If you want to do this go to **93**. If you think that it would be better to try to find a captain that can take you to Rosetta then you should head for the Captain's Bar, which is signposted just along on the right. Go to **83**.

61

Triton and his men are in sight. They haven't
spotted you yet, but you need to think fast.
You look up at where the tube connects with
the door of the ship and see that there are two
handles, one on either side. Without thinking,
you grab the first one and yank it downwards.
You then spin around and do the same with
the second. There is a creak and a groan and
then the tube comes away from the side of
the ship. A rush of air almost pulls you out
of the door, but you manage to grab hold of
a pipe.

'A spy!' screams Triton, desperately putting
on an oxygen mask as the tube bends in space,
spilling out several of his men.

Some of Triton's men are swept out into
space, others can breathe and are trying to
float towards you through the air. There is a
terrible grating sound and then an explosion.
Captain Harry's ship is on fire and is drifting
away from Triton's starship. In a second

Captain Harry's ship explodes into thousands of pieces.

You take a last look out of the open door and see Triton hanging on to a lump of metal with one hand and shaking his fist at you with the other. You hope that will keep him out of your way for a while.

With great difficulty, you struggle away from the open door and make your way down the corridor, hoping that you might be able to find a mini-ship. Turn to **19**.

62

Without a translator there is no way that you can make the starfish understand you. He calls his human friend over and whispers something in his ear.

'He wants to know who you are and what you want,' the human tells you. 'I'm his second in command and I'll translate for you.'

'I want to go to Rosetta to see my uncle,' you lie.

'A likely story,' he replies. 'No one wants to go to Rosetta. It is a miserable place – there's a plague there. Why do you really want to go there?'

Will you tell them about your mission? If so, go to **8**. Or will you decide not to tell them? If so, go to **71**.

63

Triton's three agents spot you. If you don't make a decision now you'll be trapped in the shop and they will grab you.

Will you take your chance now and run? If so, go to **47**. Or do you think that it would be safer to surrender to them? If so, go to **2**.

64

'How close to Rosetta can you take me?' you ask the stranger.

'I'll take you down to the planet myself,' he replies, already turning away and heading towards the place where his ship is docked.

When you see the man's ship you wonder how on Earth it could ever fly through space. It is battered, dented and looks as if it is only fit for the scrapyard.

'Oh, don't worry about how my ship looks,' smiles the man. 'It works perfectly. My name is Harry, by the way, but everyone calls me Captain Harry.'

In a few minutes the ship is ready to blast off from the space station. One of Harry's crewmen shows you to a bedroom, which is comfortable enough but quite dirty. You lie down on the bed and nod off to sleep. When you wake up you find yourself floating in the air and your nose is rubbing against the ceiling of the room.

Have you got a pair of magnetic boots on your feet? If you have the boots on, go to **40**. If you have not got the boots on, go to **70**.

65

The sun is beating down on you and you wish you'd brought water, but there is no time to think about that. The colony should be some distance ahead.

Suddenly, you hear a whirring sound. In the haze ahead you see a shape beginning to form. It is a truck that appears to be speeding towards you. It seems to float above the surface of the planet and doesn't need wheels. But who is in it? Do you think you should run towards the truck and see who is driving it? If so, go to **87**. Or do you think that you should hide behind a rock in case it is Triton or some of his men? If so, go to **94**.

66

The space stations and spaceships should have oxygen, which you need to breathe in order to live. But the mask will be very useful if you have to venture into space or if the oxygen fails on a spaceship.

'I'll take the oxygen mask,' you say.

'Yes, that's a good choice. You can never quite be sure whether or not there will be oxygen,' replies Colonel Strong.

You pull on a jumpsuit and zip it up. It has many pockets, which you fill with the items you need to take. Carefully you put the plague cure in one of the top pockets and zip that up. You then safely place the oxygen mask into another pocket. Colonel Strong then passes you the chip locator, which  you put into another pocket.

You are now ready to go and it will soon be time for the rocket to blast off and take you into outer space. Now go to **79**.

67

You find a side room with a door that has a round, glass window. It is dark inside the room and nobody can see your face as you look out to watch who might pass by.

'Thank you, Captain Harry. You've done extremely well and you'll be paid for your work,' announces a booming voice.

You then hear footsteps getting closer and see Triton, whom you recognise from the photo, with his arm around Captain Harry's shoulders. They seem to be extremely good friends. Behind Triton and Captain Harry are several other creatures that look exactly like Triton. They are all carrying heavy blasters and look ready for any action.

You wait for Triton's men to pass and then sneak out into the corridor, heading for the tube. Standing on guard beside the door is a large, purple creature. It has three heads and instead of arms it has tentacles, like an octopus. There are funny shaped hands

at the end of each of them and they all
hold a gun.

Do you want to try and talk to the alien? If
so, go to **55**. If you want to try and get past him
into the tube, go to **42**.

68

You walk away from the main door and hope
to find where the luggage is being unloaded.
Up ahead you can see huge conveyor belts with
all manner of boxes and cases slowly moving

out of the ship. There are plenty of workmen around but they all seem to be very busy and they don't spot you jumping onto the conveyor belt and hiding behind an enormous box marked 'Pluto'. You stay hidden behind the box until you get into Jupiter station itself. You then jump off into a crowd of aliens.

You need to find a ship to get you to Rosetta. There is a security guard up ahead; you could ask him. If you wish to do so, go to **93**. On the other side of the enormous hall is a flashing sign that reads 'The Captain's Bar'. Perhaps you might find a real captain in there that might be going to Rosetta? If you want to try the Captain's Bar, go to **83**.

69

You dive behind a hospital bed and see a gun lying on the floor. It must be Triton's. Will you grab it? If so, go to **28**. Or will you continue to hide? If so, go to **99**.

70

By grabbing hold of pipes you manage to get out of the room. You have to float along the corridor; it is hard work. Someone must have turned off the gravity. Suddenly you hear a clicking sound and the fans in the wall stop. Someone has turned off the oxygen!

Did you bring an oxygen mask with you? If you brought the oxygen mask, turn to **14**. If you did not bring the oxygen mask with you, turn to **4**.

71

You walk away for a moment, just to have a think. The starfish is deep in conversation with the human. You are not sure whether you can trust either of them, so you decide to make up a story about why you need to get to Rosetta.

'All right then: my uncle's got some valuable gems hidden on the planet and he has asked me to collect them for him. I'll let you have some of them if you take me there,' you lie.

Judging from their reaction, this seems to have done the trick. The human smiles, whispers in the starfish's ear and they both stand up.

'The captain says you can come with us, but we'd want half of the gems,' the human tells you.

'OK,' you say.

With that, the three of you leave the Captain's Bar and head for the starfish's ship. Now go to **81**.

72

Gradually, Triton overpowers you and pins you to the ground. Suddenly strange shapes pass before your eyes and you feel yourself falling, falling, falling.

You find yourself on the floor of the time chamber and see Colonel Strong's face peering through the glass. Your mission is over. Strong promised that you would not come to any harm and he has kept his promise. The colonel opens the door and helps you to your feet.

'It seems I've failed,' you say. 'I tried to handle Triton myself but he was too strong for me. We could try it all again, couldn't we?'

If you would like to try the mission once again, go back to **1**.

73

'Gulp, bibble, babble, gulp,' is the noise the frog creature makes.

You smile and look down to see that it is carrying a bag with a large sticker on it, saying 'Jupiter'. This must be a school trip to Jupiter. You continue walking with them for a while, until you reach the check-in desks. The alien children are led away by their teachers and once again you are alone. Now turn to **97**.

74

You fire straight at the alien ship, but you miss
it. By the time your blaster rays reach its
position it has moved. The enemy has already
managed to hit your ship several times and it is
swinging around to fire again. What will you
do this time? Will you fire ahead of the alien
ship? If so, go to **50**. Or will you fire straight at
it again? If so, go to **57**.

75

You turn into a passageway and only a few
metres ahead is what looks like a hospital.
There is a broad-shouldered man leaning over
one of the patients. He is wearing a white coat
and he looks like a doctor. You immediately
run up to him.

'I've got the cure to the plague,' you tell him,
taking out the test tube and showing it to him.
The man turns and smiles but you do not like
the expression on his face.

'I suppose you think I'm here to save these people?' he says. 'I'm not. I work for Triton.'

You are shocked. What will you do? Will you shout for help? If so, go to **43**. Or will you run? If so, go to **54**.

76

You try as best you can to hide in the milling mass of aliens and slowly shuffle towards the exit door. Once outside you are in a huge, domed space and hundreds of people are heading for the conveyor belt to collect their luggage.

The three alien agents are close behind you. You do not have much time. Do you want to head straight for the docks, where all of the starships are parked, and hope that you might find someone going to Rosetta? If so go to **49**. If you think it might be safer to go straight to the security police and tell them that you are being followed then go to **96**.

77

The hand with which Triton is holding the gun starts to shake and then he starts coughing so much that he just can't stop. Several of his men have appeared at the doorway and they are all coughing too.

'Poison … you've … put … poison … into … the … air,' Triton splutters as he coughs. Whatever the cure was, it has worked on the humans and, better still, it has given some kind of plague to Triton and his men.

'I … need … to … warn … everyone,' says Triton to his men. He is trying to reach for his communicator. Will you try to stop him? If so, go to **26**. Or will you try to grab his time chip? If so, go to **41**.

78

Luckily you have your magnetic boots so you will be able to get to the mini-ship. At the air lock you shake hands with Simon and wave a goodbye to the starfish. You begin your slow walk along the metal corridor. Turn to **59**.

79

With your last preparations completed, you leave the room with Colonel Strong and jump back into Harris's jeep. He drives you straight to the rocket. It is enormous.

'This is the Ariane 5. We've set up the time machine inside. I'll be coming with you and so will Harris and two of the scientists. We need to get to an exact position that is 800 kilometres from Earth. That position should let you land inside the orbiting space city 600 years into the future,' the colonel tells you.

Being a F.E.A.R. agent is exciting enough, but now you are having the chance of going

into space! You are just a little bit scared, but you are ready for anything.

A lift takes you all to the top of the rocket and you step inside. The rocket is exactly like the ones you've seen on television. All around you are computer screens, switches and dials. There are lights flashing and you can hear a constant chatter from Mission Control, who are checking that all of the systems are working.

Colonel Strong straps you into a seat and then sits down beside you. The other men are also ready and the door slams shut. You hear the lift motor fading away.

'Ready Mission Control,' says Colonel Strong.

'Check. Ignition in ten seconds,' announces a voice.

You count down in your mind and hear a roaring sound. Then the rocket begins to lift off at an incredible speed. Strong tells you that it is travelling at 11,000 metres per second. In what seems like only a few minutes, the main rocket boosters fall away and the spaceship is out of the Earth's atmosphere. You can just see the darkness of space through the window.

'OK, let's get into position,' says Colonel Strong.

The scientists make their last preparations as Colonel Strong steers the spaceship to the exact location.

Strong gets up and unfastens your seatbelt. He leads you over to the time machine.

'We're ready to send you on your mission,' he says to you. 'I'm told that the journey through time feels rather like falling. You might feel a little bit sick, but you can't come to any harm. Be careful of Triton's spies,' Colonel

Strong warns you. 'They are everywhere, some are human and some are alien. Swallow this locator chip so we can track you at all times. I promise you that you won't come to any harm. If you are ever in any real danger we'll bring you straight back.'

You shake hands with the colonel, then step inside the time chamber and take a deep breath. Suddenly the chamber feels as if it is spinning around and around. The control room of the spaceship is swirling and fading and different shapes are appearing in front of your eyes. You hear a strange, whooshing sound – like a strong wind. You keep spinning and then you feel yourself falling. Now turn to **34**.

80

'Which way to my room?' you ask the half-man, half-horse alien.

'Just press the top of your key and it will tell you which way to go,' he replies.

You follow his instructions and the key says 'Take corridor 4'. You look up and see a sign marked 'Corridor 4' and begin walking towards it. You seem to have been walking for ages before the key talks to you again. 'Take the next turning on your right, into Corridor 4a,' it says. You look behind and see that the three aliens are still following you.

Up ahead is a group of around 20 humans hanging around in the corridor. Do you want to try and hide amongst them? If so, go to **35**. Or do you want to continue on towards your room? If so, go to **10**.

81

The three of you walk along through the dock area of the space station. It doesn't look as if you are being followed, and anyway you feel safe with your new companions.

'Do you realise how dangerous this is going to be?' says the human, who by now has told you his name is Simon. 'We have to pass through pirate territory and I've heard that there is a creature called Triton who has got starships in the area and is attacking everything.'

'Really?' you ask. 'Who's Triton?'

'Let's just say he's bad – no, he's worse than bad.'

Eventually you reach Bay 97, where the starship is docked, and to your horror you see a very battered and scratched starship. You hope that you've made the right decision to travel on this to Rosetta.

Once you are onboard, you see that the ship looks great from the inside and everything works.

The starfish turns on the engines and after the spaceport's control room has told them that everything is clear, the ship roars out through an enormous gate and into space.

You have not been travelling for long when Simon tells you that the ship is being followed. You can see a large starship in the shape of a dart a short distance behind you. It must be Triton's agents!

Will you tell the captain to speed up and get to Rosetta as soon as possible? If so, go to **30**. Or do you think that the ship should try to find a different route to shake off Triton's agents? If so, go to **16**.

82

You make a sprint for the cave. It is dark and gloomy inside and you've barely walked ten metres when you nearly trip over someone lying on the floor. A light flickers on and you see a horrible sight. There are dozens and dozens of humans lying on the floor, all seriously ill

with the plague. Perhaps they have come down
to these caves to stay out of the sun? They are in
a bad way and you need to find a doctor as soon
as possible to hand over the cure. Turn to **20**.

83

As you walk into the Captain's Bar you can
barely hear yourself think with all the loud,
thumping music. The place is packed with an
even wider variety of aliens. Some are short,
some are tall, and they appear in every colour
you could think of. You walk up to the bar and
order a soft drink, then sit down and wonder
what to do next.

'So, you're off to Rosetta,' you hear. You
spin around and see a scruffy-looking human
talking to a creature that looks like an orange
starfish.

'Can I get you another drink?' says the
human to the starfish.

The starfish makes a weird sound and you
see the human making his way to the bar.

Now is your chance, the starfish is alone. Do you want to ask it whether it will give you a lift to Rosetta? If so, turn to **29**. If you would prefer to follow it when it leaves the bar then turn to **32**.

84

You look this way and that, hoping to find something to stop Triton. Then suddenly you see a huge water tank. Perhaps if you can smash the tank the water will rush through the city and sweep away Triton's tanks?

It is very risky, but if you want to try this then go to **23**. If you think that you would be better off trying to find a doctor, go to **75**.

85

Before you can get to the ticket office you have to pass through a security gate. A creature that looks like a human, except that he has two heads – one on top of the other – guards the gate. Close to his bottom mouth he has a microphone and on the top of his other head he has two small speakers.

'Move along please. Passengers flying to destinations outside of the galaxy must show their galactic passports here. All other passengers pass through the gate,' he shouts.

As you reach the security guard he puts out his hand and touches you on the shoulder. 'Anything to declare? Are you carrying

anything that you shouldn't be carrying?'
he asks.

Without waiting for you to answer he starts waving a wand around you. It makes a weird, clicking sound. Immediately you are worried that he might find the plague cure.

Will you try and hide the test tube behind your back? If so, go to **27**. Or will you leave it in your pocket? If so, go to **39**.

86

'Are – you – a – human?' asks the frog creature.

This sounds weird because the alien is talking in a different language and its voice is coming out of the universal translator.

'Yes I am. Where are you going?' you ask.

'Jupiter – adventure – holiday. We've – got – to – do – homework – though,' it replies.

'That's tough,' you say.

By now, the alien teachers have led the children past the ticket desk. No one has stopped you, asked you for a ticket or even counted the number of children. The teachers have already disappeared through a door that has been slid open and the children are beginning to follow them through.

'What's your name?' you ask.

'Gerda,' it replies.

The two of you step through the doorway and part of the floor lifts up and whisks you along a corridor and down a tube, towards another door. This one must lead onto the starship. You take a look behind you and can see that the three aliens are still following you. Now turn to **51**.

87

As you get closer to the truck you can see a green figure sitting beside the driver. It must be Triton. You wonder how on Earth he got here so fast and how he has managed to find you. You are not sure whether he has spotted you yet, so there is still a chance to get away. Do you want to run away towards a huge pile of rocks? If so, go to **5**. Or do you want to still try to get to the colony? If so, go to **38**.

88

With great luck your mini-ship is not spotted as it speeds away from Triton's starship.

'How long will it take to get to Jupiter?' you ask the computer.

'Seven hours, thirty-two minutes and fourteen seconds,' it replies.

'Is there food onboard?'

'Yes, what do you wish to eat?' it asks you.

'Burger, chips and a chocolate milk shake,' you reply, suddenly feeling very hungry indeed.

'Confirmed. Open door number seven,' the computer instructs you.

You open the hatch door and inside is a huge burger, a mountain of chips and the biggest chocolate milk shake you have ever seen.

After you have eaten you nod off to sleep. You are woken by the computer, which announces that you will be docking at the Jupiter space station in two minutes. Popping a cold chip into your mouth, you watch through the window as the huge spaceport gets closer and closer. The mini-ship parks itself inside the station and you step out, thanking the computer for a safe journey.

Now all you need to find is a ship that will take you to Rosetta. Turn to **60**.

89

'Quick! Somebody help me!' you shout.

Several of the men, that only minutes ago were lying on the ground, moaning and groaning with the plague, jump to their feet and start tackling Triton's henchmen. Two of them grab Triton himself and pin him against the wall.

You slip your hand inside his pocket and pull out his time chip. You drop it to the floor and grind it under your foot. Turn to **100**.

90

You climb up the ladder into the gun turret, sit behind the gun and hunt for the button to turn it on. Finally you find it, and the gun powers up just in time. The asteroid is only metres from you when you fire. There's no chance of missing it, and it shatters into millions of pieces.

'Great shot! That's saved us!' says Simon. 'Stay where you are, we're coming out of the asteroid belt and Rosetta is just ahead.'

You look out into space, but instead of seeing Rosetta you spot something else. An alien ship is swinging into view and firing straight at you.

'We've got company!' you shout. 'I bet it's Triton.'

The alien ship gets into range. Will you fire straight at it? If so, go to **74**. Or will you fire just ahead of it? If so, go to **50**.

91

You put on your oxygen mask, shake hands with Simon, wave goodbye to the starfish and then climb aboard the mini-ship. You press the starter button and a computer screen flickers into action.

'Destination?' it asks.

'Take me down to the surface of Rosetta.'

With that the mini-ship's engines blast off and you whizz into space. You are moving at a

terrific speed and in seconds Rosetta is in front of you.

The mini-ship flies through the atmosphere, through the clouds and then you can see the rocky surface of the planet beneath you. Will you try to land close to the colony, even though this means that you will land on very rocky ground? If so, go to **17**. Or will you land further away on flatter ground? If so, go to **46**.

92

Without the translator you've got no hope of understanding what the computer is telling you. You press all of the buttons, hoping that something will work. But it just keeps repeating the same message.

You take a quick look behind and see that Triton is leading two huge henchmen through the rocks towards you. Will you run for it? If so, go to **21**. Or will you try to hide in the doorway? If so, go to **44**.

93

You walk up to the security guard. He is a human with a pointy beard and sharp blue eyes. He seems very bored and is yawning.

'Excuse me, can you tell me how I can get to Rosetta please?' you ask politely.

'You don't want to go there. It's a bad, horrible place, full of disease. No one is allowed to go there,' he warns you.

Not very helpful, you think, so the only choice really is to go and see if you can find a real captain in the Captain's Bar. Go to **83**.

94

You manage to duck behind a huge rock just in time. The truck sweeps by and you can see, sitting in the passenger seat, the figure of Triton. You wonder how he managed to find you so easily. Maybe it is time to confront him? If you want to do that, go to **18**. Or if you think it would be better to run and try to get away, go to **5**.

95

'I'm sorry, I'm not coming with you – but thanks for the offer. I'll make my own way,' you tell him.

'I think you're mad. Your only chance of getting to Rosetta is with me,' he says.

You walk away, but turn back to look at the man and see he is talking into something that looks like a futuristic mobile phone. He is obviously telling someone something and you think that someone might be Triton. You remember Colonel Strong's warning that Triton has spies everywhere. Perhaps you were right not to trust the stranger. Now go to **37**.

96

The three aliens try to close in on you, but they back off as soon as they see the 'Security Police' sign. You turn and smile at them before you walk in the door. To your horror there is a creature that looks like Triton sat at the desk.

'Yes?' he booms.

'I'm being followed. There are three men, well, creatures, outside and they have followed me all the way from the space station that is orbiting Earth,' you explain.

The creature stands up and walks over to you. He reaches into his pockets and quickly pulls out a pair of handcuffs. In a second he snaps them onto your wrists.

'I've been told to look out for suspicious humans. Those men are probably plain-clothed security and that's why they've been trailing you. You're under arrest.'

With that he grabs you by the arm and locks you away in a cell. Before the door is even closed you see strange shapes pass before your eyes and you feel yourself falling, falling, falling.

You find yourself on the floor of the time chamber and see Colonel Strong's face peering through the glass. Your mission is over.

Strong promised that you would not come to any harm and he has kept his promise. The

colonel opens the door and helps you to
your feet.

'It seems I've failed. Some of the security
police must be working for Triton. But we could
try it all again, couldn't we?' you ask the
colonel.

If you would like to try
the mission once again,
go back to **1**.

97

You still haven't bought a ticket, so that's the
next thing you must do. But you take a quick
look over your shoulder and see three odd-
looking aliens walk past the security guard.

They won't dare attack you here, not with so
many people around. So you walk up to the
ticket desk and hand your payment card over
to a pink alien, who has green spots and
splodges all over her face.

'Where to, dearie?' she says.

'Jupiter please,' you smile.

'I've put that on your card. Just head for Gate 562,' she replies.

You thank her and head off towards the boarding gate. Now turn to **11**.

98

You need to find somewhere safe to hide, so you walk a little further along the corridor and see an open door. You look inside and see several of Triton's men opening boxes. They are all wearing masks and seem to be pouring a liquid into the top of a small missile. Perhaps the liquid is the plague and this is how they have been infecting Rosetta? The men seem to have finished their work because they close the boxes and load them onto a cart. You can only assume that they are getting them ready to take onto Captain Harry's ship.

The men must be stopped. Will you try to do something to stop Triton's evil plan now? If so go to **22**. If you think you need to make sure that the settlers on Rosetta are safe first then you need to try to find a mini-ship to get off Triton's starship. Go to **19**.

99

You decide to continue to hide and although Triton is coughing and spluttering he manages to grab the gun. He staggers towards you and raises the gun at you. His finger begins to squeeze the trigger and suddenly strange shapes pass before your eyes and you feel yourself falling, falling, falling.

You find yourself on the floor of the time chamber and see Colonel Strong's face peering through the glass. Your mission is over. Strong promised that you would not come to any harm and he has kept his promise. The colonel opens the door and helps you to your feet.

'It seems I've failed. If only I'd been able to get to the gun. I nearly had him. But we could try it all again, couldn't we?' you ask the colonel.

If you would like to try the mission once again, go back to **1**.

100

Triton's body starts to fade and he disappears.
Your mission is at an end and you have saved
the colonists.

Suddenly you feel yourself falling, falling,
falling.

You find yourself on the floor of the time
chamber and see Colonel Strong's smiling face
peering through the glass. You have barely
struggled to your feet before the colonel is
inside the chamber helping you up.

'Well done!' says the colonel, slapping you
on the back.

You are back on the rocket and everyone is
clapping and cheering.

Your F.E.A.R. mission has been a success.
You can now return home, pleased with your
work, until the next time of course. Who knows
where Triton will strike again?

The Emerald Pirate

Triton has become the Emerald Pirate! His crew are robbing and sinking ships, collecting a vast pile of gold and treasure, but why?

YOU are sent back in time to the peaceful island of Santa Diana, known to be the Emerald Pirate's next target.

Can YOU save the islanders, battle with zombies and put a stop to the Emerald Pirate's evil plan? Solve the puzzles and find the clues in this exciting adventure into a strange pirate world.

£4.99   ISBN 1 84046 690 1

The Spy Master

Triton has become Gary Steel – a criminal mastermind!
He has kidnapped the inventor Albert Fudge and is
forcing him to build the ultimate computer to take over
the world.

Can YOU discover Steel's secret base and destroy the
computer? YOU solve the puzzles and find the clues in
this exciting adventure into the world of spies.

£4.99   ISBN 1 84046 692 8

The Crime Lord

Triton has become the Crime Lord of London! His army of child thieves are robbing the capital. Even the best police detectives are powerless – they need help.

YOU are sent back into the foggy streets of Victorian London to solve the baffling case and bring Triton's grip on the city to an end. Can YOU discover Triton's secret lair? Can YOU stop him? Solve the puzzles and find the clues in this exciting adventure.

Published March 2006

£4.99   ISBN 1 84046 693 6

Fighting Fantasy™

Fighting Fantasy™ is a brilliant series of adventure gamebooks in which YOU are the hero.

Part novel, with its exciting story, and part game, with its elaborate combat system, each book holds many adventures in store for you. Every page presents different challenges, and the choices you make will send you on different paths and into different battles.

Magic and monsters are as real as life in these sword-and-sorcery treasure hunts which will keep you spellbound for hours.

There are over 20 *Fighting Fantasy™* titles available.

Click on www.fightingfantasygamebooks.com to find out more.

Suitable for readers aged 9 and upwards.

Fighting Fantasy™
The Warlock of Firetop Mountain

Deep in the caverns beneath Firetop Mountain lies an untold wealth of treasure, guarded by a powerful Warlock – or so the rumour goes. Several adventurers like yourself have set off for Firetop Mountain in search of the Warlock's hoard. None has ever returned. Do you dare follow them?

Your quest is to find the Warlock's treasure, hidden deep within a dungeon populated with a multitude of terrifying monsters. You will need courage, determination and a fair amount of luck if you are to survive all the traps and battles, and reach your goal – the innermost chambers of the Warlock's domain.

£4.99   ISBN 1 84046 387 2

Suitable for readers aged 9 and upwards.

Fighting Fantasy™
Eye of the Dragon

In a tavern in Fang, a mysterious stranger offers YOU the chance to find the Golden Dragon, perhaps the most valuable treasure in all of Allansia. But it is hidden in a labyrinth beneath Darkwood Forest and is guarded by the most violent creatures and deadly traps.

To begin your quest YOU must drink a life-threatening potion, and to succeed you must find maps, clues, artefacts, magic items, jewels and an imprisoned dwarf.

£4.99   ISBN 1 84046 642 1

Suitable for readers aged 9 and upwards.

Football Fantasy

Football Fantasy is a stunning new series of football gamebooks in which YOU decide the outcome of the match. YOU see what a footballer would see and make the decisions he would make.

Simple to play and challenging to master, every game is different. Learn the tricks and tactics of the game and lead your team to victory.

All titles £5.99

Thames United	ISBN 1 84046 598 0
Mersey City	ISBN 1 84046 597 2
Medway United	ISBN 1 84046 599 9
Trent Albion	ISBN 1 84046 590 5
Bridgewater	ISBN 1 84046 609 X
Clyde Rovers	ISBN 1 84046 621 9
Avon United	ISBN 1 84046 622 7
Tyne Athletic	ISBN 1 84046 596 4

Suitable for readers aged 10 and upwards.